seasons
of her heart

companion to *RedeemHer Heart*

Seasons of Her Heart

© 2021 RedeemHer Heart

ISBN 978-0-6451447-0-3

COVER, ILLUSTRATION & TEXT DESIGN BY Jazmin Welch
EDITED BY Siena Johnstone

All rights reserved. No part of this publication may be reproduced, stored in a retrieval system or transmitted in any form or by any means—electronic, mechanical, photocopying or otherwise—without the prior written consent of the author.

THIS JOURNAL BELONGS TO

....

....

intention

After releasing my personal memoir, *RedeemHer Heart*, the feedback I received was overwhelming with deep resonance and relatability. It became evident to me that my outpourings onto the pages of RedeemHer Heart was calling for a companion. A sacred reflection space where you can journey alongside me, experience your own remembrance and pen your own heart's seasons.

Introducing *Seasons of Her Heart*: A personal space for you to discern God's unique seasonal movements in your life and how it's significance bears on you. A journal for your heart's writings and your soul's scripts of faith.

There is no doubt that the universal principle of Seasons is interwoven in the DNA of planet Earth. These Seasons God created is nature's daily occurrence. Our journey in this life, our relationships with God, ourselves and others, all revolve around seasonal patterns. If you're not aware or paying attention, you can miss the seasonal processes of the Spirit and the many blessings that accompany them. These seasons impact everything in our lives;

From what I have come to experience, observe and recognise, there are four seasons that we find ourselves in. This journal has been divided into these four seasons: Growing, Pruning, Wilderness & Harvest. Each season holds within it gentle prompts to guide you in moving through your own life journey. This sacred space is yours.

No matter in what season you find yourself, my prayer is that in this sacred process of journaling you receive every promise and provision released by His supernatural grace.

When you accept the fact that sometimes seasons are dry and times are hard and that God is in control of both, you will discover a sense of divine refuge, because the hope then is in God and not in yourself.

—**CHARLES R. SWINDOLL**

growing (pains)

As long as the earth endures,
seedtime and harvest, cold and heat,
summer and winter,
day and night will never cease.

—GENESIS 8:22

Growing is naturally a season of change. Change is rarely easy and often accompanied by resistance which can be painful. This poses challenges, such as experiencing life in ways you have never known or seen before. Change is often new territory, it will feel foreign, with no reference points, so deeply uncomfortable, with stuck feelings of confusion where all you see are barriers and hurdles. With growth, there comes a lot of stretching. Stretching is often a form of enlarging your capacity. What can seem like failure and discomfort is simply growing pains. This season calls for deeper trust in your growth. It's taking place even if you have no evidence of that yet, keep going. Keep *growing*.

The Lord makes firm the steps of the one who delights in him; though he may stumble, he will not fall, for the Lord upholds him with his hand.

—PSALMS 37:23,24

pruning

There is a time for everything, and a season for every activity under the heavens.

—ECCLESIASTES 3:1

Pruning: reducing, shedding and altering. This will be where the testing phase comes in and God is allowing test after test to happen in your life. This is the preparation season that needs to happen for the next season to follow. This work must be completed in order for you to transition into the next season. The pruning analogy is exactly that, letting go and cutting off; of things, people and beliefs that will no longer serve you or be of help and support in the seasons to come.

These trials will show that your faith is genuine. It is being tested as fire tests and purifies gold— though your faith is far more precious than mere gold. So when your faith remains strong through many trials, it will bring you much praise and glory and honor on the day when Jesus Christ is revealed to the whole world.

—1 PETER 1:7

wilderness

For everything there is a season,
yet God has made everything beautiful
for its own time.

—Ecclesiastes 3:11

Wilderness is a season of dryness, waiting, lack and even suffering. This season can be perceived as the loneliest time in one's life. Feeling totally out of step and in misalignment with God, yourself and others stems from feeling like your circumstances no longer match up with what you believe to be true about God and life in general. You can't feel, see or hear him anymore. God appears to go silent and you begin to doubt everything and everyone, detaching and falling into deep darkness and despair. The wilderness is harsh and lonely. It will call from your patience like never before, and in this time, believe it or not, God is the most nearest to you. Press in!

*The Lord is near to the brokenhearted
and saves the crushed in spirit.*

—PSALM 34:18

harvest

*For there is a proper time and
procedure for every delight,
though a man's trouble is heavy upon him.*

—ECCLESIASTES 8:6-7

You will be reaping the benefits and ripe fruit, gathering the labour of the seeds you had planted and sowed in your previous seasons. In reference to the farmers harvest this signifies a very busy period, demanding a lot of your time, energy, strength and devotion. With this, overwhelm often seeps in. It will call from you again to deeply trust that you have developed the maturity and capacity to undertake the big work before you, because God entrusts you with much. It may be a struggle to stay on track pressing into God because the fruit is sweet and everything is going well but don't forget the lessons you overcame in previous seasons. The harvest is the anticipation of God's abundant, provisional blessings.

For I am sure of this very thing, that the one who began a good work in you will perfect it until the day of Christ Jesus.

—PHILIPPIANS 1:6

www.ingramcontent.com/pod-product-compliance
Lightning Source LLC
Chambersburg PA
CBHW022019290426
44109CB00015B/1228